I0415470

Raising A Child With Autism

Understanding The Puzzle

© **Copyright 2019-20 Arden Marketing Enterprises - All rights reserved.**

In no way is it legal to reproduce, duplicate, or transmit any part of this document in either electronic means or in printed format. Recording of this publication is strictly prohibited and any storage of this document is not allowed unless with written permission from the publisher. All rights reserved.

The information provided herein is stated to be truthful and consistent, in that any liability, in terms of inattention or otherwise, by any usage or abuse of any policies, processes, or directions contained within is the solitary and utter responsibility of the recipient reader. Under no circumstances will any legal responsibility or blame be held against the publisher for any reparation, damages, or monetary loss due to the information herein, either directly or indirectly.

Respective authors own all copyrights not held by the publisher.

Legal Notice:
This book is copyright protected. This is only for personal use. You cannot amend, distribute, sell, use, quote, or paraphrase any part of the content within this book without the consent of the author or copyright owner. Legal action will be pursued if this is breached.

Disclaimer Notice:
Please note the information contained within this document is for educational and entertainment purposes only. Every attempt has been made to provide accurate, up to date, and reliable complete information. No warranties of any kind are expressed or implied. Readers acknowledge that the author is not engaging in the rendering of legal, financial, medical, or professional advice.

By reading this document, the reader agrees that under no circumstances are we responsible for any losses, direct or indirect, which are incurred as a result of the use of information contained within this document, including, but not limited to, —errors, omissions, or inaccuracies.

Table Of Contents

Introduction 6
Chapter 1: Autism Spectrum Disorder 7
  1.1 What Is An Autism Spectrum Disorder? 7
Chapter 2: Autism Affects For Children 10
  2.1 Affecting Attention And Interaction.........................10
    2.1.1 Regulation And Control.....................................11
    2.1.2 Only Seeing Details 12
Chapter 3: Cure For Autism 13
  3.1 Occupational Therapy...13
Chapter 4: The Signs Of Autism 16
  4.1 Warning Signs 16
  4.2 Stimming 17
  4.3 Correlation Between Autism And Pretend Play 18
    4.3.1 Exploratory Play 19
    4.3.2 Cause and Effect Play 19
    5.3.3 Functional Play 20
    4.3.4 Constructive Play...20
    4.3.5 Physical Play...20
    4.3.6 Pretend Play 21
Chapter 5: Other Medical Conditions Encountered By Autistic Children 22
  5.1 Co-Occurring Conditions 23
    5.1.1 Gastrointestinal Disorders (GI) 23
    5.1.2 Epilepsy 24
      5.1.2.1 Major Red Flags 24
      5.1.2.2 Less Specific Red Flags...............................24
    5.1.3 Eating and Feeding Issues 25
    5.1.4 Disrupted Sleep...25
    5.1.5 Attention Deficit and Hyperactivity Disorder 26
Chapter 6: Triggered Depression For Parents With Autistic Children 27

6.1 Handling Emotional Strain 29

6.2 Importance Of Looking At Your Child As A Hero.................30

   6.2.1 Brutal Honesty 30

   6.2.2 Fearless 31

   6.2.3 Quietude..31

   6.2.4 Solitude 31

   6.2.5 Routine..32

Conclusion 34

Introduction

I want to thank you and congratulate you for downloading *Raising A Child With Autism*. This book will help inform you on many aspects of Autism Spectrum Disorder. It is a complicated neurological disorder that even the most educated scientists and researchers have not been able to fully understand yet.

This book contains proven steps and strategies on how to become a truly knowledgeable parent for a child who needs extra love, time, and attention. However, this does not outweigh the love that they return to you.

Here's an inescapable fact: you will need to understand autism, as well as cherish the differences. Just as other children, those with autism are just as different and unique with a special sense of love and triumph with every goal met.

If you do not develop your patience and understanding right off the bat, then do not feel as if you failed. It is not just a neurological disorder, but it is a lifestyle. Lifestyles always take time to learn and adapt to.

It's time for you to become a prepared advocate for your amazing and unique child.

Chapter 1: Autism Spectrum Disorder

Surprisingly enough, even though the numbers are climbing, there are many who are unsure of what Autism Spectrum Disorder really is. Those in the mental health industry are more aware of the symptoms of Austin Spectrum Disorder, also referred to as ASD.

The increasing number does not mean that more people are developing this mental disorder, but instead, more are becoming aware of it. It is due to the knowledge we now know and being able to catch cases in children.

1.1 What Is An Autism Spectrum Disorder?

An Autism Spectrum Disorder (ASD) is a highly complex developmental condition. It involves consistent challenges in speech, interactions in social settings, and nonverbal communication. It also restricts and is the cause of repetitive behaviors.

The severity of ASD symptoms differs from person to person. Just like snowflakes and neurotypical people, those with autism are extremely unique.

Due to the wide range of symptoms, this specific condition is labeled Autism Spectrum Disorder. It is a type of umbrella term due to the differences in each and every single person. It ranges anywhere from slightly affected in social matters all the way to impairment of typical living and may include institutional medical care.

Children that have autism experience many issues when it comes to communicating with other people. They have a difficulty understanding what others may be thinking or feeling.

It can make it even harder to effectively communicate their own feelings and thoughts. Many times these children have an extremely hard time communicating what they need.

There have been a number of genes that show association with autism. Imaging studies of those who have autism show that there are differences in the development of different regions in the brain. There are studies that suggest that autism is a result of disruptions in the child's normal brain development early on in the developmental stages.

The disruptions may be the effects of genes that are in control of brain development, as well as regulate how their brain cells communicate. Autism cases are found more so in cases where the child was born prematurely.

Some environmental factors may also be responsible for gene function, as well as development; however, there are no specific environmental causes identified as of yet. The theory of that states parental practices are the cause of autism has been disproved. There are many studies showing that vaccinations as previously thought are not the cause, nor do they increase the risk of developing autism spectrum disorder.

Studies done on families and twins show that some people have a genetic predisposition to this disorder. Identical twin research and studies show that if one of the twins are affected by autism, then the chance that the other will have autism ranges between 36 percent to 95 percent.

When it came to families that included a child that has an autism spectrum disorder, it was found that the parents of one autistic child would have an increased risk of having a second child with an autism spectrum disorder. Numerous genes that are responsible for autism are also involved in the chemical connections between the brain and the neurons. Researchers are still working hard to pinpoint specific genes.

Chapter 2: Autism Affects For Children

Children that are diagnosed with ASD will develop at different rates than each other, as well as their peers. This does not necessarily mean they will not develop the skills. It also needs to be stated that most children will not develop the skills in the same order either.

For instance, a child with autism may begin to use a few words singularly when they are about twelve months old. This same child may only use a few new words per month and not have a language explosion until they are three years old.

Another autistic child may be able to label their own body parts, but they may not be able to label the same body parts in a children's picture book. They may be able to label colors but not put them together in a pile with the same color. For instance, separating clocks by color. This is all different per child with autism.

2.1 Affecting Attention And Interaction

Those with autism do not tune into the surrounding others in the same way neurotypical people do. For example, a child with autism may not respond to their name, smile at their caregivers, make appropriate eye contact, or even wave goodbye without prompting. An autistic child may also not use their finger to point for attention or for communication.

Children with autism also have issues with joint attention. It can make it difficult for a child to develop language and communication skills. For instance, if one parent is pointing to a specific picture of a dog, but this child is looking elsewhere, it will be hard for the child to learn that there is a link between the picture and the word "dog".

Those children with autism find it difficult to see things in the perspective of someone else. They may have issues understanding the desires or the beliefs of another person. They may also find it difficult to understand or predict the behavior of another person.

Seeing things from another person's view is crucial when it comes to social skills. Without this, a child with autism will find it difficult to make friends and get along with others.

Neurological children will learn these skills around three to five years old; however, those with autism will develop these skills later.

2.1.1 Regulation And Control

Children on the spectrum will struggle with attention, focus, transitions, memory, organization, emotional control, time management, and frustration. We need these abilities to survive our everyday lives.

A child with autism will find it difficult to learn due to this symptom of autism. It can affect learning how to solve math problems. The child may know the facts, but may not be able to come up with the solution. They are unable to organize their thoughts or ideas to solve the problem.

2.1.2 Only Seeing Details

It is difficult for a child with autism to see the 'big picture'. They will get lost in all the details instead of seeing the situation in its entirety. They will not be able to see 'the forest through the trees'.

This issue will make it difficult for the child to develop and learn. They will have poor reading comprehension. They may only remember a few small details and forget the meaning of the story they heard or read.

There are more difficulties for these special children to overcome, but keep in mind that with help they are able to function. Just because they have autism does not mean that they are not happy and healthy. They just need to learn how to functioning heir own in society, and that is where you come in as a parent.

Chapter 3: Cure For Autism

Many people want to find a cure for autism; however, at this point in time, there is no cure. Scientists believe that there are two reasons for the development of autism, which are environment and genetics. Although stated previously, it should be stated again that it has been disproved that the environment has been linked to autism.

If there is no cure, then how can one with autism recover?

There is no recovery; however, there is a way to navigate a life having autism. This includes different types of therapies. These therapies are performed by trained and educated professionals. It is said that the earlier a person with autism is able to receive these therapies; the more functions the person will be able to perform, as well as cope with throughout their life.

The types of therapies and methods have a very large range; however, Occupational Therapy is a definite constant when it comes to getting help for those with ASD.

3.1 Occupational Therapy

Those with autism, as well as Attention Deficit Hyperactivity Disorder, tend to show significant patterns that are different from a neurological child. Their process patterns dealing with sensory is so much different than their peers, along with other special needs children.

It has been estimated that 60 percent to 70 percent of those with ASD show sensory modulation. Studies show that those with autism are slower when it comes to integrating inputs that are coming in from the senses, which makes their process time much slower. It is to be said that this is a big part of the autistic child having 'meltdowns'.

They lack the right 'filters' that screen out the irrelevant information and this leads to the meltdown as each of the inputs build up. They are still processing it just as others are coming in at the same time and it is overwhelming. An example of this is a loud noise in the hallway from ten minutes ago, and now something new is going on.

An overload of the senses is presented in different ways like behavior, shutdown, or withdrawal. However, there are many easy strategies that are able to be utilized in the classroom and at home in order to add in the sensory filters.

Occupational therapists are crucial to this type of intervention. Adding the correct type of filters for your child, along with intervention, will allow your child to help overcome their jittery nervous system.

Occupational therapists help to promote, develop, and maintain certain skills that are needed by children in order to function in a school setting and more.

Active occupational therapy participation helps to promote:

- Self-esteem

- Learning

- Self-confidence

- Social Interaction

- Independence

This type of therapy is to be considered a type of holistic program. The therapist will take the physical, emotional, social, cognitive, and sensory abilities of each and every single child. They will concentrate on fine motor skills, handwriting, and everyday living functions.

Chapter 4: The Signs Of Autism

Autism Spectrum Disorder ranges in signs from person to person, as well as severity. Many people with ASD even have a different combination of signs. There are no two children that are alike. The symptoms of ASD can be mild or severe, and often times will change over time.

One thing that most parents are not familiar with is the fact that under federal law a child that is suspected of having a developmental disorder is able to get a free evaluation. It is recommended by the American Academy of Pediatrics to have your child screened for any developmental conditions or disorders before the age of three.

If you have suspicions or any concerns that your toddler is developing behind their peers, then it is crucial that you bring this up with your child's pediatrician. There are different red flags that should be paid attention to, especially when it comes to time-sensitive conditions, like autism.

4.1 Warning Signs

- The child not responding to their name by the age of twelve months.

- If your child is not pointing at different objects to show their interest in the age of fourteen months old.

- If your child is not playing any pretend games by the age of eighteen months.

- If they avoid eye contact or if they prefer to be alone.

- Your child will display agitation if there are minor changes to their environment or routine.

- Most children with autism will have a 'stim'. This includes the stereotypical stem-like flapping. They may rock their body or even spin in circles.

- Your child may have an unusual or even intense reaction to the way some things taste, smell, feel, and look.

If your child has any of these signs, then you should speak to your pediatrician. Most doctors will also have information on hand about autism and will gladly give you copies.

Take this home and read them. They may even have a questionnaire in order to help evaluate if this is something that may be a cause for concern.

4.2 Stimming

To be straight forward, stimming is defined as a behavior that is culturally unacceptable. For example, it is normal to see a person biting on their nails or twirling their hair in their fingers; however, it is not acceptable to see one go about flapping their hands around.

Occasional or mild rocking is typically acceptable; however, rocking the entire body is considered to be stimming. Flapping may be one of the typical types of stims, but there are others that are a lot less acceptable in society than flapping.

Some autistics will make really loud noises that can either sound scary or even threatening. There are some who hit themselves or even hit their head on a wall. This type of stim is very problematic for different reasons, mainly due to them hurting themselves.

For most people who have autism, stimming will occur once in a while. However, there are times that they may find it extremely hard to stop stimming. They may even do it for the entire day.

Most adults with autism are aware of their stimming and can control it for the most part. This goes right back to the benefits of Occupational Therapy.

Those with autism will typically stim when they feel happy, anxious, excited, overwhelmed, or when it will comfort them. Under certain stressful situations, they may even stim for longer periods of time.

Although some autistics can control or are aware of their stemming, there are others that are not. They do not understand the reactions of others. They may not be able to control it or at least find it very difficult to resist the urge.

4.3 Correlation Between Autism And Pretend Play

Pretend play helps develop fine motor skills, gross motor skills, communication skill, language skills, problem-solving, as well as social skills.

Those on the spectrum are impacted by not being able to pretend play appropriately. However, with therapies, a child with ASD is able to develop the appropriate skills and learn to cope with the symptoms of ASD.

Children with autism enjoy playing; however, they do have difficulties with certain types of play. They normally do not like to play in a spontaneous way.

You will probably see your child play in a repetitive type of way or have only a few toys that are deemed their favorites. For instance, you may see your child finish a puzzle in the same exact order every time they put it together.

Since autism affects the development of communication and social skills, it may also affect the development of the skills needed for play, like the ability to share objects, explore their environment, take turns, and to respond to their peers.

Here are the types of play so that you can build a foundation of routine for play for your child at home.

4.3.1 Exploratory Play

The child will feel, look, and even mouth objects. You will need to encourage the child to explore the many different objects around them. You can splash water in your bathtub or give them a sensory toy. Having a lot of floor time is important.

4.3.2 Cause and Effect Play

The child with ASD will play with different toys that will require action in order to produce the desired result. An example of this is pressing a certain button to play music. This toy offers a sense of control.

You will need to praise the child when they do it right. This will encourage them to perform the correct actions. Utilize this type of toy and play in order to teach them to take turns and follow instructions.

5.3.3 Functional Play

This type of play is where the child with autism utilizes a toy in the right way. For example, running a toy car across the floor instead of throwing it across the room. You need to engage in the play with your child in order to show them how to use the toy functionally. Join in with their play first, then direct them to utilize the toy in the right manner.

4.3.4 Constructive Play

This is where the child will make or build things that involve working towards a specific goal. An example of constructive play is to put a puzzle together or making a tower. Some autistic children may have delays in this type of play. You are able to encourage this type of play by modeling this type of play.

4.3.5 Physical Play

This specific type of play offers your child a chance to grow their gross motor skills. You are able to help the child by participating in physical play.

You need to start at a young age and engage in active games together. While there are some children that do not like to be tickled, there are other types of physical play like 'Simon Says' or 'hide-and-seek'.

4.3.6 Pretend Play

It has been shown that pretend play is directly associated with verbal skills. This is where your child will "make-believe". For instance, your child may pretend that their toy spider jumped on their head and now they are in fear of being bitten.

This play is often times delayed in those with autism. However, there are many children that are able to develop pretend to play skills and those who have verbal communication issues will soon begin to develop them.

Chapter 5: Other Medical Conditions Encountered By Autistic Children

Most parents that are new to having a child with autism do not know that along with ASD, your child is subject to other conditions that come along with autism.

Over half of those that are on the spectrum will have four or more conditions. These types of conditions are co-occurring and how they come about will vary from one child to another.

These co-occurring conditions can, and times do, exacerbate the features that are included with autism. Understanding how they will interact with the ASD diagnosis is pretty crucial.

Here are the conditions that have been found to be linked to autism.

- Epilepsy

- Attention Deficit Hyperactivity Disorder

- Obsessive Compulsive Disorder

- Depression

- Fragile X Syndrome

- Tuberous Sclerosis Complex

- Anxiety

- Sleep Conditions

Different characteristics and genetics play a role in which of the issues that the child may encounter. For instance, sleep issues will affect between forty-four percent to eighty-six percent of children on the spectrum.

Characteristics that affect the conditions include age, race, gender, and intelligence quotient. It is to be noted that if the child is non-verbal autistic, it may be hard to diagnose a mood disorder, like anxiety.

5.1 Co-Occurring Conditions

There is a large range of mental and physical health conditions that are included with an Autism Spectrum Disorder diagnosis. In this section, you will learn not just about some conditions, but other information to look for when you have a child that has ASD.

5.1.1 Gastrointestinal Disorders (GI)

These disorders are eight times more common in children with ASD than their peers. They include:

- Abdominal Pain

- Chronic Constipation

- Gastroesophageal Reflux

- Bowel Inflammation

5.1.2 Epilepsy

This disorder is a seizure disorder that affects close to one-third of those with autism. It only affects one to two percent of the neurotypical population.

5.1.2.1 Major Red Flags

- Involuntary Movements

- Unexplained Staring Spells

- Severe Headaches

5.1.2.2 Less Specific Red Flags

- Disrupted Sleep

- Sleepiness

- Unexplained Changes in Emotions or Abilities

Treatment of this condition is important in order to prevent damage to the brain. If you suspect that your child may have this condition, you will need to see a neurologist immediately.

5.1.3 Eating and Feeding Issues

Eating and feeding issues affect seven out of ten children that have autism. These problems may include restricted habits with food, as well as aversions to specific textures and tastes.

There are many adults that have ASD that describe their aversions to food. This challenge typically stems from hypersensitivities and the need for sameness.

Another eating issue is overeating. This will lead to obesity. It typically stems from the inability to feel 'full' when they are eating. Eating is a sensory behavior that helps sooth the body. Those with this issue will need therapies to ensure that their health stays intact.

Pica is another eating disorder that many children that have autism suffer with over their life. It is dangerous due to children eating things that are not food.

Children with autism typically like to chew and eat paper. This is one of the most common items. There are products like pencil chews and necklace chews that are made of hard rubber and safe for this type of stim.

5.1.4 Disrupted Sleep

Over half of those with autism have issues with sleep. No matter if the person is a child or an adult, the sleep problems exist. It will interfere with their learning and decrease the quality of life of this person overall. Most pediatricians will suggest a natural sleep aid and tips on putting them on a sleep schedule.

5.1.5 Attention Deficit and Hyperactivity Disorder

ADHD affects thirty to sixty percent of those with autism. However, in the general population, it only affects six to seven percent. This condition involves a pattern on difficulty remembering things, inattention, trouble managing time, hyperactivity, impulse control issues, and other issues in their daily life.

It is to be said that the symptoms of ADHD and autism overlap. Due to this issue, it is hard to distinguish between the two conditions at times. Anxiety disorders affect approximately forty-two percent of those with autism. In the general population, it only affects about three percent in children and only fifteen percent in adults.

Since those with autism have issues expressing and assessing how they feel, this behavior often shows that they are experiencing anxiety. Anxiety can trigger muscle tightness, racing heartbeat, and more. Some people can even feel like they are frozen in place.

Another form of anxiety is social anxiety. It is the fear of crowds, new people, and situations that prove to be too social. This is a big concern with those on the spectrum. Children with autism have a hard time fighting their anxiety due to the symptoms of ASD.

Chapter 6: Triggered Depression For Parents With Autistic Children

Before we go into *'why'* on anything, it needs to be said that if you are experiencing depression after your child's diagnosis, it is normal. You do not have to feel guilty about feeling sad and depressed.

Yes, your child was diagnosed. Yes, you have a right to your feelings even though it was not you that received the diagnosis personally.

The University of North Carolina conducted a study that included mothers with children on the spectrum. It was found that fifty percent of the mothers were found to be depressed due to feeling as if it were their fault.

It was also found that fifteen to twenty-one percent of the group were depressed about the situation even though they did not feel responsible. Mothers that were single were subject to severe depression.

The feeling of being never enough, or even good enough, will lead to depression. In some cases, individual counseling for mothers is needed. However, while the feelings of inadequacy and guilt are definitely in their minds, there is so much more to the entire story.

The families with children on the spectrum, even those that are higher functioning, face many different obstacles in everyday living and it is a struggle. These struggles lead to feelings of frustration, irritability, anger, anxiety, and more.

Here is a list of different feelings that you may have after a diagnosis:

- Those who are receiving a diagnosis for their child will be coping with the loss of their expectations for their children and for parenthood. At the very same time, they are losing out on typical children things like playdate and other things like sports activities.

- It can be extremely hard to engage in a typical social activity with an autistic child. Social isolation becomes an issue. You cannot take your sensory sensitive child to Little Timmy's musical clown, balloon popping, music ridden birthday party.

- It is expensive to treat a child that has ASD. There are many families that go into deep debt in order to support the therapies that insurances do not cover. This will lead to depression, anxiety, and anger.

- Many mothers end up quitting their jobs in order to stay home to care for their child with ASD. They then lose those connections at work with people they socialize with, they lose the money that they were earning, and they are now alone.

- One thing that every parent with an autistic child knows is that with ASD comes a very large issue with sleep. Most children with ASD keep their parents up most nights. This will lead to exhaustion with depression not far behind.

- Those parents who have to fight with the public school system and the mental health agencies for the appropriate services are at high risk of developing depression.

- As the child grows older, the parent then will face "retirement" with the financial responsibility of a child that is an adult. They depend on their parents for everything.

Having a child with ASD does lead to depression; however, the specific reasons differ. No matter how hard you try to be optimistic, your mind is racing and always planning. It is exhausting and hard. Make sure to take care of yourself as well. If you do not then you cannot take care of your child.

6.1 Handling Emotional Strain

Coping is a skill that is taught and learned as a child, which your child will be learning through Occupational Therapy. Sometimes what we know to do just is not good enough, like in this case. You would have never planned on having a child with this disorder; therefore, you would not know how to cope without the proper tools to do so.

Here are some ideas when you are facing emotional strain:

- Find some support with like-minded people that have children that are on the spectrum.

- Get respite care so that you are able to get a break when you feel like you are on the edge.

- Seek out professional help from a therapist of your own. Make sure they are familiar with working with parents that have children on the spectrum.

- Writing in a journal in order to get the thoughts out of your head is a good idea. This is done in many different types of therapies for many different types of situations.

- Try to find a way to lower the cost of the therapies.

- Most of all though, just know that you are doing the best you can with what you have. It is a parent's nature to always feel like there is more they can do.

6.2 Importance Of Looking At Your Child As A Hero

When we all speak about autism spectrum disorder, we end up focusing on the negative. We focus on what needs to be fixed, modified, and addressed. Very rarely do people talk about the good that actually does come out of being autistic. A neurological person can learn a lot from someone with ASD.

Here are five aspects of being autistic that we should embrace and be proud of:

6.2.1 Brutal Honesty

It is typical for a three-year-old child to walk up to an adult without a socially acceptable filter installed. For instance, a child asking where that beer belly came from. They may even poke it.

However, it would be socially unacceptable for a teenager or adult to ask about the extra weight around your stomach. Those with autism live their life with no restrictions on honesty. We often try to live a transparent life, but we are too afraid.

6.2.2 Fearless

Parents with autistic children are very well acquainted with the term fearless. It introduces the parent to a new-found worry. Dangers do not register in the mind of a child with autism. Could you imagine being fearless? You could conquer all of your goals in life without any doubts.

6.2.3 Quietude

With today's technology and business, we are surrounded by loud, random noises on a constant basis. Some of these noises are welcome, while many others are not. This means that when the noise is turned off it is awkward and makes us feel uneasy.

Those with ASD enjoy the silence and ensure the surrounding peace. How wonderful would it be to have one afternoon where all you did was sat and relax; genuinely relax. The cut out all the excess noise and chaos.

6.2.4 Solitude

Solitude is the twin of silence. It is very hard to have one of these without the other one. Monks are known for practicing a type of silence called cooperative silence. However, they normally end up in solitude because it is much easier to achieve silence alone.

Autistic children prefer to be left alone. Humans are social animals and need the company of their peers. Watch on the television for instance. The television is the social interaction and noise that is used to ease that social side when you are alone. Those with ASD are not affected by solitude. They love it.

6.2.5 Routine

Routine is another aspect of ASD. It is not a bad trait at all. We all could learn a lot from someone with ASD. They could definitely show us the value in keeping routine. We all have been conditioned to throw things away quickly.

We have been conditioned to be wasteful. For instance, that microwave that you just threw away because you wanted a different color. Someone with ASD would have never had been so wasteful. They do not like the change, thus showing loyalty to their personal bubble.

Those with autism are heroes. Those who have autism think (differently) than others. Their peers may look at this as a disability, but if you sit back and give it some thought, those with ASD not only fight daily to maintain their life; they should be an example of how we should live in our daily lives.

.

Conclusion

Thank you for downloading this book!

I hope this book was able to help you to understand Autism Spectrum Disorder. It is a very complex neurological disorder that we are still learning about every day. Inside this book is information about autism, where to start once you get a diagnosis, and more.

The next step is to discuss any concerns with your child's primary health physician. It is crucial to catch the disorder as soon as possible. It is a time sensitive disorder.

Finally, if you enjoyed this book, please take the time to share your thoughts and post a review on Amazon. It'd be greatly appreciated!

Thank you and good luck!

Don't forget to check out Teresa's other books on Amazon.com.

Below you'll find some of my other books that are popular on Amazon and Kindle as well. Simply click on the links below to check them out. Alternatively, you can visit my author page on Amazon to see other work done by me.

https://www.amazon.com/dp/B072P62GGQ

Make Your Own Honey Mead at Home: The Homestead Series (Volume 2)

Brew Your Own Beer

The Burn Everything Cookbook: Stories and Recipe of Lean Times

Spirit Guides: Work and Bond with your Spirit Guide

How to Build a Moonshine Still plus recipes

If the links do not work, for whatever reason, you can simply search for these titles on the Amazon website to find them. Or try my Author page

The End

www.ingramcontent.com/pod-product-compliance
Lightning Source LLC
Chambersburg PA
CBHW032104280526
45784CB00013B/3117